*What You
Should Know About
Inerrancy*

What You
Should Know About
Inerrancy

by
Charles C. Ryrie

Moody Press
Chicago

All Scripture quotations are from the *New American Standard Bible,*
© 1960, 1962, 1963, 1968, 1971, 1972, 1973, 1975, and 1977 by
The Lockman Foundation, and are used by permission.

Library of Congress Cataloging in Publication Data

Ryrie, Charles Caldwell, 1925-
    What you should know about inerrancy.

    1. Bible—Evidences, authority, etc. I. Title.
BS480.R93   220.1'3   80-25257
ISBN: 0-8024-8785-8

Printed in the United States of America

Contents

Chapter One

The Dominoes
Are Falling

The Dominoes
Are Falling

Long before I knew how to play dominoes I used to play with them. I carefully set them up in rows, sometimes even with S curves. Then I would lightly tap the first one, watch the others topple, and in one brief moment destroy the fruit of my painstaking labor.

Sometimes all did not fall, and then I was very disappointed.

As I survey evangelicalism today and what is happening to evangelical doctrine, I am reminded of my old childhood game. Now I hope all the dominoes will not fall. Those doctrines that we hold dear and important to our faith are like dominoes. Each is individually important. If we remove one by ignoring or falsifying it, then the "faith which was once for all delivered to the saints" (Jude 3) is incomplete. If one falls, others

9

will inevitably be affected, and the entire structure is in danger of being demolished.

Certainly, some doctrines are more important than others. For example, without a proper doctrine of Christ, there really is no *Christian* faith. But without a reliable Bible, how can we be certain that our understanding of Christ is correct? A true doctrine of the Holy Spirit affects not only our understanding of the Trinity, but our understanding of other important doctrines such as salvation and sanctification as well. But how can we know the truth about the Holy Spirit unless we can trust the accuracy of the Bible? If the Bible accommodates in the area of science, for instance, then perhaps it accommodates also in what it teaches about the Spirit.

If all the doctrines of the Bible were like dominoes standing in a line, then obviously the credibility of the Bible would stand first in line. Whether the first domino stands or falls inevitably affects some, most, or even all of the others.

Is that domino falling today? The attack on the total accuracy of the Bible is coming not from liberals but from born-again believers who call themselves evangelicals, yet do not believe in the inerrancy of the Scriptures. Certainly, that domino is teetering. For some it has already fallen.

What about the other dominoes? Are other doctrines being affected? Belief about the Bible assumes a place of primary importance in one's doctrinal system. If the Bible does in fact teach its own inerrancy, then to deny that doctrine is to disbelieve the Bible. If we cannot trust the Bible in a fact of history that seems unrelated to any major doctrine, how can we be sure we can trust it in a matter of history, like the empty tomb, which

10

is unquestionably related to a very major doctrine? How can anyone who lets the domino of inerrancy fall be sure that it will not knock over some other doctrine as well?

Chapter Two

So Many Words

So Many Words

To affirm clearly one's belief in the inspiration of the Bible demands many words today. That was not always so. Formerly, it was enough to say, "I believe in the inspiration of the Bible." That said it all. Everyone understood those words to mean that the Bible was from God, completely accurate and reliable, and therefore authoritative.

Verbal inspiration. Later, it became necessary to add, "I believe in the verbal inspiration of the Bible." *Verbal* emphasized the fact that the very words were inspired, not only the thoughts, as some were saying. If only thoughts are inspired, they said, there can be considerable freedom in the choice of words to express those thoughts; thus, they concluded, "It is not possible to speak about the inspiration of the words of the text of Scripture." But those who held to full inspiration of words as well as thought insisted that God must have guided the very words used by the writers, or the Bible is less than inspired. Hence the phrase "verbal inspiration" seemed necessary.

15

Verbal, plenary inspiration. But some sought to undermine inspiration by asserting that although words might be inspired, not all of them were. They insisted that there was no way to claim that every word in the Bible was inspired. So to affirm inspiration it became necessary to add, "I believe in the verbal, *plenary* (complete, full) inspiration of the Bible." That assured that no part of the Bible would be omitted.

Verbal, plenary, infallible inspiration. In time another attack on the complete inspiration of all the Bible was launched. Some denied that the Bible, though "inspired," was infallible. Then it became necessary to say, "I believe in the verbal, plenary, *infallible* inspiration of the Bible." That affirmed that the words were exactly the ones God wanted in the text, and therefore every word was authoritative.

Verbal, plenary, infallible, inerrant inspiration. Nevertheless, some could not accept the idea that the words were exactly those God intended, and yet they were reluctant to abandon the authority of Scripture. So there developed the attempt to allow for errors in the text while keeping the "infallibility" of the message. To counter that, it became necessary to say, "I believe in the verbal, plenary, infallible, and *inerrant* (without error) inspiration of the Bible." Adding the word "inerrant" focused on the necessary relation between accuracy of the words and authority of the message.

Verbal, plenary, infallible, inerrant, unlimited inspiration. Today there has appeared yet another attempt to undermine full inspiration. The new doctrine affirms belief in inerrancy but limits the extent of inerrancy. The Bible, they say, "is inerrant when it speaks of science, history, or genealogies, and so on." In other words, it possesses only "limited inerrancy."

But why say "limited inerrancy"? Why not "limited errancy"? If the Bible has limitations on its inerrancy, then obviously it is errant, though not completely so. So limited inerrancy and limited errancy amount to the same thing. But why do the proponents of limited inerrancy not want to use the equivalent label "limited errancy"? One cannot be sure of the answer, but it could hardly be denied that limited inerrancy is a much more palatable label than anything that has the word *errancy* in it. What evangelical would not want to avoid using a label that suggests he believes that there are errors in the Bible? To speak of limited inerrancy seems much more respectable, but it is also more deceitful. Intentional or not, it is a semantic game played to help cover up a dangerously deceptive view. We need to expose limited inerrancy for what it is. If parts of the Bible are not inerrant, then those parts are errant. That is an inescapable conclusion.

Therefore today, "in order to affirm clearly a belief in the full inspiration of the Scripture," it has become necessary to say, "I believe in the verbal, plenary, infallible, unlimited inerrancy of the Bible."

Is the question of inerrancy truly important? Many are saying no, but others insist that inerrancy is a crucial doctrine. Some try to drive a wedge between parts of the total affirmation; others insist the whole statement stands or falls together. Is this a major issue or not? To help answer the question we need to examine some of the excuses offered for not accepting a doctrine of inspiration that includes inerrancy.

Chapter Three

Some Excuses

Some Excuses

Some say the inerrancy is either unimportant, irrelevant, or unnecessary to the faith. Therefore, all the furor being stirred up over it is merely a tempest in a teapot, and those who insist on it are disturbing the peace of the church.

But that simply is not so. Inerrancy is a crucial issue, for if the Bible is not completely without error, then it must have at least one error in it. Now if we could all agree on where that one error is, the problem might conceivably be tolerated. But, if current literature is any guideline, there would be about twenty candidates for that "error," and that means there might be as many as twenty errors. And if there could be as many as twenty errors, then the question becomes: How can I trust the Bible at all? Inerrancy is not a tempest in a teapot.

Several reasons are commonly offered for concluding that inerrancy is a nonessential doctrine.

Those who oppose or who want to diminish the importance of inerrancy often make the statement: "Inasmuch as the Bible does not clearly teach iner-

21

rancy, neither can we." At the very least that places those who insist on the importance of inerrancy in the position of insisting on more than the Bible does. At the most, it implies or asserts that inerrancy is not a biblical doctrine.

But for the statement to be true requires (a) that we can show that the Bible does not clearly teach inerrancy, and (b) that if it does not, in the sense of providing proof texts, we cannot assert inerrancy on the basis of an inductive study of the evidence. Let us examine those requirements.

Does the Bible clearly teach inerrancy? The answer will depend on what is meant by "clearly." If by "clearly" one means proof texts such as those present in the Bible for substitutionary atonement, for example (Matthew 20:28), then admittedly there is not that type of "clear" evidence for inerrancy. But many doctrines for which there are no proof texts are accepted by evangelicals as being clearly taught in the Scriptures. The doctrine of the Trinity furnishes the best example of that. It is fair to say that the Bible does not clearly teach the doctrine of the Trinity, if by clearly one means there are proof texts for the doctrine. In fact, there is not even one proof text, if by proof text we mean a verse or passage that "clearly" states that there is one God who exists in three persons.

How then do we arrive at a doctrine of the Trinity? Simply by accepting two lines of evidence in the Bible: (1) clear statements that teach there is only one God: and (2) equally clear statements that there was someone called Jesus and someone designated the Holy Spirit who in addition to God the Father claimed to be God. Such evidence permits only one of two conclusions: either Jesus and the Holy Spirit are not divine, or God exists as a triunity. Orthodox Christians have never shied away from the second conclusion even though

22

evidence for it is of a different kind of clarity than that which proof texts provide.

Or, to take another example, many deny that Jesus is God because, they say, there is no "clear" evidence that He ever claimed to be divine. Robert Alley, then of the University of Richmond, stirred up a furor among Southern Baptists when he asserted that Jesus "never really claimed to be God or to be related to him" ("Some Theologians Question Factual Truth of Gospels," *Richmond News Leader,* 17 July 1978, p. 1). Even though he possessed the same evidence from the Bible as those who conclude that Jesus did claim to be God, he arrived at a completely different conclusion. The "proof texts" commonly used by evangelicals did not for him clearly teach the deity of Christ. Such heresy outrages orthodox believers, and rightly so.

Though I have not yet discussed the evidence for the clear teaching of the Bible as to its own inerrancy, let us assume for the moment that it does teach it clearly, though not necessarily by proof texts. If so, are errantists demanding of the Bible a higher standard of clarity to prove inerrancy than they require to prove the deity of Christ or the Trinity? In other words, do they not have one set of criteria for clearly proving the doctrine of the Trinity and another for inerrancy?

The above illustrations prove the fallacy of concluding that if something is not "proof texted" in the Bible, we cannot teach the results of an inductive study or reach logical conclusions drawn from the evidence that is there. If that were so, I could never teach the doctrines of the Trinity, the deity of Christ, the deity of the Holy Spirit, or even forms of church government.

Often I hear people say, "I will go only as far as the Bible does." That can be a good standard, because we do not ever want to add to what the

Bible teaches. But neither do we want to omit anything it teaches whether by clear proof texts, clear deduction, clear induction, clear implication, clear logic, or clear principles. The claim for not wanting to go beyond what the Bible teaches can be merely an excuse for not wanting to face the implications of what it does teach. And I fear that for some that has been their excuse for not wanting to face what the Bible does say about its own inerrancy.

A second excuse for diluting the importance of inerrancy is that since we do not possess any original manuscripts of the Bible and since inerrancy is related to those originals only, the doctrine of inerrancy is only a theoretical one and therefore nonessential. It is true that we do not possess any of the original manuscripts of the Bible, and the doctrine on inerrancy, like inspiration, is predicated only of the original manuscripts, not on any of the copies. The two premises in the statement above are correct, but those particular premises do not prove at all that inerrancy is a nonessential doctrine.

Obviously, inerrancy can be asserted only in relation to the original manuscripts because only they are the original record of what came directly from God under inspiration. The very first copy of a letter of Paul, for instance, was in reality only a copy and not the original that Paul himself wrote or dictated. Both inspiration and inerrancy are predicated only on the originals. But would an errantist claim that *inspiration* is a nonessential doctrine, on the basis of not having the originals, and not attributing inspiration to the copies? I think not. Then why does he say that about inerrancy?

Another argument is that inerrancy is a recent teaching about which the church formerly was not

24

concerned; therefore, we need not be so concerned today.

The argument from church history seems to rear its head almost every time any doctrine is discussed. If the doctrine was taught in ancient times, it is supposedly more reliable. If, on the other hand, it has not been taught until more re-cent years, then it is suspect.

Of course, the argument itself is invalid. The truth or untruth of any doctrine does not depend on whether or not it was ever taught in church history. Its truthfulness depends solely on whether or not it is taught in the Bible. Now, ad-mittedly, a teaching that no one has ever before heard about might be suspect, but the Bible, not church history, is the standard against which all teachings must be measured.

Nevertheless, the history excuse persists with the doctrine of inerrancy. It is recent, they say, Therefore the debate should cease.

Some say inerrancy originated with B. B. War-field at Princeton in the late 1800s. Others claim that Frances Turretin, a Lutheran theologian, started it all just after the Reformation.

Actually neither man did. We believe that Christ taught inerrancy as well as did the apostle Paul. Furthermore, Augustine, Aquinas, the Reformers, and other great men held to it throughout church history. Granted, such evidence from history does not validate the doc-trine (Christ's and Paul's teaching do, and we shall examine that later), but it invalidates the claim that says inerrancy is a recent invention.

For example, Augustine (A.D. 354-430) clearly stated:

> Most disastrous consequences must follow our believing that anything false is found in the sacred books: that is to say that the men

by whom the Scripture has been given to us and committed to writing, did put down in these books anything false. If you once admit into such a high sanctuary of authority one false statement, there will not be left a single sentence of those books, which, if appearing to anyone difficult in practice or hard to believe, may not by the same fatal rule be explained away as a statement, in which intentionally, the author declared what was not true. [*Epistula,* p. 28]

Here in ancient terms is the same domino theory mentioned earlier.

Again, Thomas Aquinas (1224-1274) plainly said, "Nothing false can underlie the literal sense of Scripture" (*Summa Theologica* 1. 1, 10, ad. 3). Also, Luther declared, "I have learned to ascribe this honor, i.e., infallibility, only to books which are termed canonical, so that I confidently believe that not one of their authors erred" (M. Reu, *Luther and the Scriptures,* p. 24). Again, "The Scriptures have never erred" (*Works of Luther,* XV: 1481). John Wesley, the founder of Methodism, wrote, "Nay, if there be any mistakes in the Bible there may well be a thousand. If there is one falsehood in that book it did not come from the God of truth" (*Journal* VI: 117).

How can anyone say, then, that inerrancy is a recent invention?

But even if it were, it could still be a true doctrine.

Only the Bible, not history, can tell us.

Chapter Four

What Does Inerrancy Mean?

What Does Inerrancy Mean?

Definitions of inerrancy are not plentiful! Many errantists equate inerrancy with infallibility, and then limit its scope to matters of faith and practice or to revelational matters or to the message of salvation.

"The Bible is infallible, as I define that term, but not inerrant. That is, there are historical and scientific errors in the Bible, but I have found none on matters of faith and practice" (Stephen T. Davis, *The Debate about the Bible* [Philadelphia: Westminster, 1977], p. 115). At least that is an honest distinction between infallibility and inerrancy.

The Lausanne Covenant declared the Bible to be "inerrant in all that it affirms." The phrase is admittedly flexible, since it may allow for errors in areas like creation where, according to some interpreters, the Bible is not affirming historical facts. Both inerrantists and errantists could subscribe to that statement.

The International Council on Biblical Inerrancy in its Chicago statement affirmed inerrancy in a brief statement that the "Scripture is without error or fault in all its teaching." Then followed nineteen articles to further describe and explain inerrancy.

That brief statement, unlike the Lausanne declaration, would be unsatisfactory to errantists. If there were any doubt about that, certainly the nineteen-article elaboration would exclude errantists' agreeing with it.

The dictionary defines inerrancy as "being without error." Most definitions of inerrancy share that negative description. The question raised then by that definition is, What is error? Can the Bible use approximations and still be without error? Can a New Testament writer quote freely from the Old Testament and claim that the resultant quotation is without error? Can a biblical writer use the language of appearances without communicating error? Can there exist different accounts of the same event without involving error?

Admittedly, the data of Scripture often includes approximations, free quotations, language of appearances, different accounts of the same occurrence. Can that data support a definition of inerrancy as "being without error?" Obviously, the data and the definition must harmonize if that is a correct definition of what the Bible teaches about its own inerrancy.

Perhaps the tension would be erased if we defined inerrancy positively—the inerrancy of the Bible means simply that the Bible tells the truth. Truth can and does include approximations, free quotations, language of appearances, and different accounts of the same event as long as those do not contradict. For example, if you were to report to me that a mutual friend had a

30

hundred-thousand dollar income last year, I might well say (especially if I had never considered him to be a rich man), "Are you telling me the truth?" When you reply, "Yes," that would be an inerrant reply, even though his income for reporting to the Internal Revenue Service was $100,537. That approximation would tell the truth.

Or if I said, "Sunrise over the Grand Canyon is one of the most spectacular sights I have ever seen." And if you replied, "Really, is that so?" to which I said, "Yes, that's true," my statement with its own use of language of appearance would tell the truth, although the sun does not literally rise over the Grand Canyon.

Does the Bible say not to lie? Yes, it says do not lie. Is that a true statement? Of course, though it is also true (but not more true) to say that the Bible says, "Lie not one to another." But the free quotation tells the truth.

Or again, my wife told me that when she saw the changing of the guard at Buckingham Palace, a soldier fainted and fell on the ground. But the newspaper reported that on the same day *three* men fainted. That was also a true report. If my wife had said that *only* one man fainted, her report would have been wrong. Actually three did, but she focused only on the one nearest to where she was standing. She may even have noticed that the others also fainted, but simply did not report that. Nevertheless, her statement was true.

If 1 Corinthians 10:8 says 23,000 died in one day and Numbers 25:9 records 24,000 but does not add the restriction "in one day," we understand both to be telling the truth (and probably both figures are approximations of the number that died in one day and the number of additonal deaths later).

31

If a New Testament writer makes a free quotation from the Old Testament, since he was writing under the inspiration of the Spirit, that free quotation becomes part of the inspired, inerrant text. The Holy Spirit, the author of both Old and New Testaments, certainly has the right to quote Himself as He wishes and to use quotations with meanings we as uninspired interpreters might never have seen.

Using the language of appearances is a common way of communicating, sometimes even more vividly than scientific language could.

If Mark and Luke speak of only one blind man given sight at Jericho, whereas Matthew reports two, both statements are true as long as Mark and Luke do not say *only* one man.

Most debates over truth and error get off track when they become philosophical and not down to earth. Most people understand clearly and easily that approximations, and so forth, tell the truth. The Bible is inerrant in that it tells the truth, and it does so without error in all parts and with all its words.

If it were not so, then how could the Lord affirm that man lives on *every* word that proceeds from the mouth of God (Matthew 4:4), especially if all Scripture is breathed out by God (2 Timothy 3:16)?

Chapter Five

Inerrancy and the Character of God

Inerrancy and the Character of God

Though most often connected with the doctrine of inspiration, 2 Timothy 3:16 also says something important about inerrancy. The reason ought to be obvious: inspiration and inerrancy are interrelated.

Inspiration wrestles with the question of how God gave us the Bible. Did He dictate it to men? If so, then a correct understanding of inspiration says that God gave us the Bible by dictating it. That is the view that many liberals ascribe to evangelicals, and a few evangelicals do hold it (though denying it is mechanical dictation). "God raised up men, prepared the men and prepared their vocabularies, and God dictated the very words which they would put down in the Scriptures" (John R. Rice, *The Sword of the Lord,* 10 January, 1975, p. 14). However, most who hold to inerrancy reject dictation, asserting that God guided and guarded the human authors to record His message without dictating it.

Or, on the other end of the scale, did God do nothing more special than give the world men of great genius who produced the Bible just as other geniuses have written great books? That view is labeled natural inspiration. "But the line of demarcation between it and other religious writings . . . is not so sharp and final as to establish a qualitative difference between all other writings and every part of the canonical Scriptures" (Cecil J. Cadoux, *A Pilgrim's Further Progress* [London:Religious Book Club, 1945], p. 11).

Or, more "Christian" than natural inspiration is the view that the writers of the Bible were Spirit-filled in the same manner that believers today can be Spirit-filled and write good books. If God gave us the Bible that way, it was more mystical than natural, though certainly not dictated.

> The inspiration of the books of the Bible does not imply for us the view that they were produced or written in any manner generically different from that of the writing of other great Christian books. There is a wide range of Christian literature from the second to the twentieth century which can with propriety be described as inspired by the Holy Spirit in precisely the same formal sense as were the books of the Bible. [Alan Richardson, *Christian Apologetics* (New York: Harper, 1948), p. 207]

Popular today is the idea that inspiration is not so much concerned with the character of the Bible as it is with that moment of existential revelation when something becomes truth to the individual reader. In such a concept, the Bible, of course, does not have to be inerrant. According to that idea, truth is found not in the statements or propositions of the Bible, but in subjective encounter with God's activities recorded there, often erroneously and even nonhistorically. "It is further to be noted . . . that, in the Bible, God's self-revelation is personal rather than propositional. That is to say, ultimately revelation is in relationship, 'confrontation,' communion, rather than by the communication of facts" (C.F.D. Moule, "Revelation," in *The Interpreter's Dictionary of the Bible* [Nashville: Abingdon, 1962] 4:55).

Such a view comes close to the neo-orthodox view of the Bible, which sees it not as revelation itself, but as a pointer or witness to revelation. Inspiration, wrote Barth, is the "act of revelation in which the prophets and apostles in their humanity became what they were, and in which alone they in their humanity can also become for us what they are" (*Church Dogmatics*, 1: 2, 563). That view proposes that the witness, the Bible, is fallible and thus often unreliable, but what it teaches is truth!

Not quite so blatant is the very comtemporary idea that the Bible's fallibility lies only in parts that do not really matter as far as salvation is concerned. It teaches that God's purpose was to give man the revelation of God in His redemptive love in Christ, and in fulfilling that purpose God saw to it that we had an infallible record. Other areas of biblical revelation, such as creation, history, or geography, which do not directly concern our salvation, may contain errors. Sometimes this view is called partial inspiration.

All those views of inspiration, except dictation, say that God gave us the Bible with errors. Inspiration answers the question, How did He give the Bible? Inerrancy answers the question, Did He give it with or without errors? Obviously, one's view of inspiration automatically contains an answer to both questions. So inspiration and inerrancy are inseparably linked, and no one can hold a view of inspiration that does not also include some view of inerrancy.

But look again to 2 Timothy 3:16. It does speak to both questions. Specifically, what facts does it tell us about the Bible?

1. *The entire Bible* was God-breathed. The Greek word here translated "Scripture" is used fifty-one times in the New Testament and always refers to some part of the Bible. Sometimes it includes the entire Old Testament (Luke 24:45; John 10:35), sometimes it refers to a particular Old Testament passage (Luke 4:21), sometimes to a particular New Testament passage (1 Timothy 5:18), and sometimes to a larger portion of the New Testament (2 Peter 3:16).

Those last two verses carry a great deal of importance. In 1 Timothy 5:18, Paul joins an Old Testament and a New Testament reference and calls them both Scripture. The Old Testament quoted is Deuteronomy 25:4, and the New Testament is Luke 10:7. It is not remarkable that an Old Testament reference should be cited as Scripture, but to join a New Testament reference with it so soon after it was written is highly significant. Probably only five or six years had elapsed between the writing of Luke and the writing of 2 Timothy, and yet Paul does not hesitate to place a quotation from Luke on the same plane as one from the accepted, canonical Old Testament.

In 2 Peter 3:16, Peter said that Paul wrote some things hard to be understood and things that some people distorted as they did other Scripture. Here, too, New Testament writings were designated Scripture and therefore authoritative. In that instance, much more than a single quotation was involved. Here, Paul's writings were called

38

Scripture.

So in 2 Timothy 3:16, Paul must have intended to include all of the Old Testament and as much of the New Testament as had been written to that time. That means that 2 Peter, Hebrews, Jude, and all of John's writings would not have been included in his understanding of "all Scripture" since they had not yet been written. Nevertheless, because those books were eventually acknowledged as belonging to the new canon of Scripture, we may safely say that the verse teaches something about the entire sixty-six books of the Bible as we know them today. Not any part is excluded; *all* Scripture is inspired of God.

Most do not debate that the verse includes all of the canon. If someone wishes to reduce the amount of Scripture included in this verse, he translates it: "All Scripture inspired by God is also profitable." In other words, whatever parts of Scripture that are inspired are profitable, but the other (uninspired) parts are not. Thus by such a translation only part of the Bible is inspired.

Is such a translation accurate?

The answer is yes.

Is such a translation required?

The answer is no. Equally correct and preferable is the translation, "All Scripture is inspired of God and is profitable."

Both translations supply the word "is." It becomes a question of whether to supply "is" only one time or two times ("Every Scripture inspired of God is also profitable," or, "All Scripture is inspired of God and is profitable"). The preference goes to the latter translation for three reasons: (a) By supplying it two times, both adjectives ("inspired" and "profitable") are understood the same way, as predicate adjectives. That is more natural. (b) The connective word ("and," or "also") is much more frequently translated "and."

39

(c) A similar construction occurs in 1 Timothy 4:4, where both adjectives are clearly predicate adjectives.

The conclusion could not be clearer: the entire Bible is inspired.

2. The entire Bible is God-*breathed.* "Given by inspiration of God" is a single Greek word, "God-breathed." The form is passive, meaning that the Bible is the result of the breath of God. If the form were, by contrast, active, then the verse would be saying that all the Bible breathes God; that is, all the Bible exudes or speaks of God. Of course, the Bible does exude God, but it is clear that Paul was saying that God breathed out the Bible.

Our English word *inspire* carries the idea of breathing into something. But here we are told that God breathed *out* something, namely, the Scripture. In other words, the origin of the Bible is God.

3. The entire Bible is *God*-breathed. Who is this God who breathed out the entire Bible? He is, among other things, truth. Not only is He true (Romans 3:4), but He is truth itself (John 14:6). Obviously, if He is truth and true, He cannot utter anything false. That is a very important consideration in answering the second question, Did God give us the Bible without errors? How could a true God do anything else? And that is why the Lord could state emphatically and without any exceptions that God's Word is truth (John 17:17).

Let us put it another way, in the form of a syllogism, a logical argument consisting of a major premise, a minor premise, and a conclusion.

Major premise: God is true (Romans 3:4).

Minor premise: God breathed out the Scriptures (2 Timothy 3:16).

Conclusion: Therefore, the Scriptures are true (John 17:17).

As any dictionary will confirm, if the premises of a syllogism are true the conclusion must also be true. We know in this syllogism that the premises are true because they are biblical statements. Therefore, the conclusion (which is also a biblical statement) is also true. Furthermore, such a conclusion is not surprising, since inspiration must also say something about inerrancy. A God-breathed Bible must be a *true* Bible. God's inspiration requires the product's accuracy.

To sum up: 2 Timothy 3:16 states three important facts about inspiration and inerrancy: (a) All the Bible is included, (b) all the Bible was breathed out from God, and (c) all the Bible is, like God, without any defects.

41

Chapter Six

Inerrancy and the Will of Man

Inerrancy and the Will of Man

No verse comes closer to telling us how God used human authors to produce the errorless Bible than 2 Peter 1:21: "For no prophecy was ever made by an act of human will, but men moved [borne, KJV*] by the Holy Spirit spoke from God." Here we are told that God the Holy Spirit carried human authors along to speak (in writing) God's message.

What was conveyed to us? The prophecy of Scripture. It is likely a reference to all of the Old Testament, not merely the parts that predicted something ahead of time. By extension we may also understand it to include the New Testament as well. All of the Bible was conveyed to us by the Spirit's working.

How was the Bible conveyed? The Spirit bore men along. What does that mean? Perhaps we

_____*King James Version.

can best understand "bearing" by referring to another use of the same word in Acts 27:15 and 17. Just before the ship that was taking Paul to Rome was wrecked on the island of Malta, it ran into a terrible storm. The experienced sailors could not guide the ship because the wind was so strong. They finally had to let the wind take the ship wherever it blew. The ship's being driven, directed, carried about by the wind, is described in these verses by using the same word as in 2 Peter 1:21 that describes the Spirit's driving, directing, carrying the human authors of the Bible as He wished. The word is a strong one, indicating complete superintending by the Spirit of all that the human authors wrote. Nevertheless, just as the sailors were active on the ship—though the wind, not the sailors, was directing the ship—so the human authors were active in writing as the Spirit directed.

But the human authors' wills did not direct or carry the Scripture. The text is clear: prophecy was never borne by the will of man (this is the same verb as in the latter part of the verse). The Spirit carried the Word, not the will of man. Man's will, including his will to make mistakes, did not bring the Scripture; rather, the Holy Spirit, who is perfect and who bore the human writers along, brought us the Scriptures. They wrote under the operation of the Spirit; therefore, those things they wrote were His, directed by His will, not theirs.

The Holy Spirit is the Spirit of truth (John 16:13). Some people affirm the truthfulness of God and yet deny the truthfulness of the Bible. They say that God is true and that anything that comes from God must also be true. But, they continue, the reason that the Bible is not true in every detail is simply that God had to involve men in

46

producing the Bible, and whenever men are involved the possibility of error creeps in. Be they ever so few, errors are nevertheless there because sinful men were used in the production of the Scriptures.

Logical as that may sound, it does not affirm 2 Peter 1:21. The human wills of the authors were not the originators or the carriers of God's message. That does not mean that the authors were totally passive (as the dictation idea of inspiration asserts), but it does mean that whatever the Spirit was and did in inspiration, their human wills were not and did not do. And the Spirit was the source and the guiding force; the authors' wills were not. The repetition of the same verb in both parts of the verse is significant ("no prophecy was *borne* ever by man's will but men were *borne* by the Spirit," author's trans.).

The conclusion is obvious: God did not permit the will of sinful man to divert, misdirect, or erroneously record His message.

Chapter Seven

What Christ's Incarnation Teaches About Inerrancy

What Christ's Incarnation Teaches About Inerrancy

The logic of some still insists that anything involving humanity has to allow for the possibility of sin. So, they say, as long as the Bible is both a divine and a human book the possibility and actuality of errors exist.

Let us examine that premise. Is it always inevitable that sin is involved where humanity is?

If you were tempted to respond affirmatively, an exception probably came to mind almost immediately. The title of this chapter put the clue in your mind. The exception is our Lord Jesus Christ. He was the God-man, and yet His humanity did not involve sin. He serves as a clear example of an exception to the logic pressed by people who believe in errancy.

The true doctrine of the God-man states that He possessed the full and perfect divine nature and a perfect human nature, and that those were united, in one person forever. His deity was not in any detail diminished; His humanity was not in any way unreal, though sinless; and in His one person His natures were without mixture, change, division, or separation.

Similarly, the Bible is a divine-human book. Though it originated from God, it was actually written by man. It is God's Word, conveyed through the Holy Spirit. Sinful men wrote that Word, but did so without error. Just as, in the incarnation, Christ took humanity but was not tainted in any way with sin, so the production of the Bible was not tainted with any errors.

Let us take the analogy further. In the humanity of Jesus Christ there were some features that were optional. He had to be a Jew. He could not have been a Gentile. He had to be a man, not a woman. He had to be sinless, not sinful. But there were some features of sinless humanity that might be termed optional. Jesus could have possessed perfect humanity within a variation of a few inches in height at maturity. A dwarf or a giant would have been imperfect. He might have varied a little in weight at maturity and still have been perfect. Surely the number of hairs on his scalp, within limits, could have been a sinless option. However, it was the humanity that He exhibited that was, in fact, perfect humanity.

The writers of the Bible were not passive. They wrote as borne along by the Spirit, and in those writings there were some things that could not have been said any other way. Paul insisted on the singular rather than the plural in Galatians 3:16. But there were, conceivably, some sinless options as in Paul's emotional statement in Romans 9:1-3. Yet the Bible we have is in fact the perfect record of God's message to us.

Everybody wrestles with the relationship between the divine and the human authors of Scriptures. The divine must not be so emphasized as to obliterate for all practical purposes the human; and the human must not be allowed to be so human as to permit errors in the text. God did dictate the law (Deuteronomy 9:10). On the other end of the divine-human involvement scale, Dr. Luke researched his material (Luke 1:1-4). Paul expressed himself freely (Romans 9:1-3), and he expressed himself rigidly (Galatians 3:16); but everywhere he wrote accurately what God wanted us to have.

A similar thing happened with regard to the person of Christ in the early centuries of church history. Docetism, a first-century heresy, taught that Christ did not actually become flesh but only appeared as a man, thus robbing Him of genuine humanity. Docetism was, of course, a Christological error, but one can see the analogy with the question of the dual authorship of the Bible. Those who hold to errors in the Bible say that inerrancy overemphasizes the divine authorship to the neglect of its "humanness." Thus God's superintendence of the Bible to the extent of producing an errorless Bible is said to be a Docetic view of inspiration. Karl Barth has made that charge, and so, more recently, have Dutch theologian Gerrit Berkhouwer and Fuller professor Paul Jewett.

But if it were true (which it is not) that those who hold to the total inerrancy of the Bible are espousing a heresy akin to Docetism, then it would be equally true that those who hold to any kind of errancy support a doctrine analagous to Ebionitism.

In the second century the Ebionites denied the deity of Christ by denying His virgin birth and His preexistence. They regarded Jesus as the natural son of Joseph and Mary, who was elected Son of

God at His baptism, but not as the eternal Son of God. They thought Jesus was a great prophet and higher than the archangels, but not divine.

Now if inerrancy is supposed to be a Docetic-like heresy, then errancy, albeit limited, is obviously an Ebionitelike heresy, since the humanity of the Bible has to permit errors in the Bible. According to the errancy view, inasmuch as real men were involved, their writings cannot be guaranteed to be without error even though the Holy Spirit directed and inspired them. That is an Ebionitelike error.

But remember, there is an orthodox doctrine of the person of Christ, and there is an orthodox doctrine of the Bible. Both involve God and man, and both result in a sinless product.

Chapter Eight

Inerrancy and the Teachings of Christ (1)

Inerrancy and the Teachings of Christ (1)

A deduction consists of a major premise, a minor premise, and a conclusion. We looked at the deductive evidence for inerrancy in chapter 5: God is true, God breathed out the Bible, therefore the Bible is true. Of course, any deduction is only as good as its premises. In that particular deduction, both premises are good and true simply because they are clearly stated in the Bible itself. So the deductive evidence for inerrancy is as strong and conclusive as the authority of the Bible itself.

But there is also another line of reasoning, the *inductive*. In an induction one reasons from parts to the whole, from particulars to the general. A conclusion is thus drawn from the evidence.

An induction is only as good as the completeness of the evidence studied. If the first five typewriters one saw were all electric, one might conclude that all typewriters were electric. Of course, the first nonelectric typewriter observed would invalidate the conclusion. But not all inductions run that high a risk of being invalid, for if one can examine as much evidence as possible, he can be assured of a very reliable conclusion.

We can examine all of the recorded teachings of Christ. We do not believe that there is any likelihood that some unrecorded teaching of Christ will turn up to invalidate the evidence we find from His teachings in the gospels. If we can investigate all that He said concerning the reliability of the Bible, then we can draw a valid conclusion about Christ's view of the Bible.

If we find that He only used or taught in a general way about the Bible, then we may conclude that He believed in its reliability generally. If, on the other hand, we find that He relied on the minutiae of the Bible as accurate, then we must conclude that He believed it to be inerrant down to its details.

Let us consider the evidence of Matthew 5:17-18: "Do not think I came to abolish the Law or the Prophets; I did not come to abolish, but to fulfill. For truly I say to you, until heaven and earth pass away, not the smallest letter or stroke [*jot or tittle,* KJV] shall pass away from the Law, until all is accomplished."

First, what is the promise? It is that the law and the prophets will not be abolished, but fulfilled. Abolish means not to accomplish something, and fulfill means to accomplish the promises. Christ is guaranteeing something about promises' not failing.

Second, what is encompassed in the promise? "Law and prophets" included all of the Old Testament, our Lord's Bible. "Law" in verse 18 means the same thing (compare the use of "law" in John 10:34, where it includes more than the Mosaic law).

Third, in what detail will all the promises of the

58

Old Testament be fulfilled? The Lord said you can count on the Old Testament promises' being fulfilled down to the very jots and tittles.

The jot is the Hebrew letter *yodh.* It is the smallest of all the letters in the Hebrew alphabet. It would occupy proportionately about the same amount of space that an English apostrophe takes up in a line of English type. Actually, the Hebrew letter looks very much like an English apostrophe. Though it is the smallest of the Hebrew letters it is as important as any other letter, for letters spell words, and words compose sentences, and sentences make promises. If you spell a word one way, it is a specific word; if you spell it another way, even only a single letter differently, it is a different word. *Tough* means strong. One letter changed spells *touch.* One letter added spells *though.* Single letters spell different words. Our Lord promised that not one jot would fail. Every promise will be fulfilled just as it was spelled out.

Observe that Christ does not start with concepts and then allow for optional words to be used to convey those concepts (as concept inspiration teaches). He begins the other way around. The promises are based on the words as spelled, and those words can be relied on fully and in detail.

Neither did our Lord say that the promises would be fulfilled provided they were culturally relevant at the time of fulfillment. In some circles today promises are culturally reinterpreted, thereby actually invalidating the original promises. But Christ taught that we could count on plain fulfillment of the original promises as spelled out in the Old Testament.

A tittle is even more minute than a jot. Whereas a jot is a whole letter, a tittle is only a part of a letter. The presence of a tittle forms a certain letter, but its absence causes that letter to become a different one. For example, the Hebrew letter *beth* looks like this: ב. The letter *kaph* looks like this: כ. Obviously they appear to be very similar. The only difference between the two letters is that the bottom horizontal line on the *beth* extends slightly to the right of the vertical line, whereas no extension appears on the *kaph*. That extension—not the entire bottom horizontal line but only the part of it that extends to the right of the vertical line—is a tittle. If it is present, the letter is a *beth;* if it is absent, it is a *kaph*. And whether you see a *beth* or a *kaph* will result in your spelling different words.

As another example, the Hebrew letter *daleth* looks like this: ד. The *resh* looks like this: ר. Again the tittle is only that part of the horizontal line that extends to the right of the vertical line. But a word spelled with a *daleth* is different from one spelled with a *resh*.

The Lord's promise was that not one jot or tittle will fail to come to pass of all the promises of the Old Testament. They are precisely spelled and thus precisely fulfilled.

In English we might illustrate a tittle this way: suppose I invite you to my house to have some *Fun*. You might rightly wonder what I consider fun. If I put a tittle or small stroke on the *F,* then you might conclude that I like to *Pun*. Punning is fun to me. There is nothing like a fast repartee of puns with someone. But you may not enjoy making puns, so I put another tittle on the letter. Now I have spelled *Run*. To run is fun for some, but not for me. So I add another tittle and now I am inviting you over to have a *Bun*. The difference between Fun, Pun, Run, and Bun is just the addition of a tittle in each case. But four entirely different words result, and with them, four distinct invitations!

60

Minutiae do make a difference. Toward the end of His earthly ministry the Lord again reaffirmed His total confidence in the minute reliability of the Scripture. At the Temple celebration of the Feast of Dedication, or Hanukkah (instituted in 165 B.C. to commemorate the cleansing and reopening of the Temple after its desecration by Antiochus Epiphanes three years earlier), the Jews asked Jesus to tell them plainly if He was the Messiah (John 10:25-39). His answer was, "I and the Father are one." The word "one" is neuter; "one thing," not "one man." In other words, He did not assert that He and the Father were identical, but that He and the Father possessed essential unity, that He enjoyed with His father perfect unity of nature and of actions. The Jews had asked if He was the Messiah. His answer was more than they had bargained for, for in it He claimed also to be equal with God.

That was certainly the way they understood His claim, for immediately they prepared to stone the Lord for what they considered to be blasphemy. In order to restrain them the Lord appealed to Psalm 82. He called that portion of the Old Testament "the law" (v. 34), as He did on two other occasions (John 12:34 and 15:25). In that law, He said, the judges of Israel, human beings, were called "gods" by virtue of their high and God-given office. Then, He concluded, if that psalm can apply the term "gods" to human beings, then certainly the term "son of God" may be rightly applied to the one whom the Father sanctified and sent into the world. In other words, if *elohim* is applied to men, how much more appropriate it is to apply it to Himself, since He does possess essential unity with the Father.

Though the argument is highly sophisticated,

61

certain claims Christ made about the Bible are crystal clear.

The Bible is verbally inspired. He pointed the Jews to what had been *written.* God's Word came in written propositional statements, not merely in concepts, thoughts, or oral tradition. It is the written record that was inspired and that can be relied on.

The Bible is minutely inspired. Psalm 82 is not what would be considered a major Old Testament passage. It is neither a psalm of David nor a messianic psalm. That is not said to demean in any way the psalm (for, of course, it is equally inspired with all other parts of the Bible), but to emphasize that the Lord did not pick an outstanding passage on which to base His argument. Indeed one might say, without being disrespectful, that He chose a rather ordinary, run-of-the-mill passage. Of course, He could not have done so if He did not believe that God's inerrant inspired Word included such passages. Furthermore, from that ordinary passage He focused on a single word, "gods." He could not have done so unless He believed in the minute inspiration of the Bible. He rightly assumed He could count on any part of the Bible and any word in any part.

The Bible is authoritatively inspired. In the midst of His sophisticated arguing, the Lord threw in almost incidentally the statement "And the Scripture cannot be broken." What does that mean? Simply that the Scripture cannot be emptied of its authority. The only way it could fail to have complete authority would be if it were erroneous, but Christ said here that it was both authoritative and inerrant. Some translations place that phrase in a parenthesis. It may be better to regard it as depending on the "if" that begins the sentence. That "if" introduces a first class condition, which

62

means certainty and is better translated "since." Thus the Lord was saying that two things are certain: the psalm called them gods, and the Scripture cannot be broken. Remember that Christ was here staking His life on the reliability of the Scripture, for His enemies were about to stone Him. Even further, He was banking on the accuracy and authority of one word of that Scripture.

Christ banked on the inerrancy of the Bible because He believed in its inerrancy. That is the only way its authority in details could be relied on. And He did rely on details—jots, tittles, and single words.

If He did, so may we. Indeed, so must we. For how can one fully follow Christ without also following His attitude toward God's Word?

Chapter Nine

Inerrancy and the Teachings of Christ (2)

Inerrancy and the Teachings of Christ (2)

Picture the scene: the Lord on "Face the (Jewish) Nation" and "Meet the (Pharisaic) Press," all in the same day. The Herodians had tried to trap Him by asking if it was lawful to pay the poll tax to Caesar. Then the Sadducees took their turn (Matthew 22:23-33). In that dialogue we have more clear evidence of our Lord's faith in an inerrant and therefore minutely authoritative Scripture.

The Sadducees believed in the authority of the Pentateuch. They denied, however, the existence of angels and other spirits and belief in the resurrection of the dead because they could not find them taught in the Pentateuch. Coming to Jesus, they immediately demonstrated their hypocrisy by posing a question about the resurrection. In addition they dreamed up an illustration based on the Pentateuch, to reinforce their question. It was

67

the law of Levirate marriage (from the Latin meaning "husband's brother's marriage," found in Deuteronomy 25). The law required the brother-in-law of a childless widow to marry her if he were able to do so. If not, then the responsibility fell on his next of kin as in the story of Ruth and Boaz (Ruth 4:6).

It was on that basis that the Sadducees concocted a story about seven brothers, the first of whom married a woman and died leaving her childless. Then each of the other six married her in turn after each of his older brothers died. Finally, the seventh husband died, and last of all the wife.

The Sadducees confronted the Lord with their question: "In the resurrection therefore whose wife of the seven shall she be? For they all had her."

His answer was scathing. He charged them with error, with ignorance of the Scripture, and with ignorance of the power of God (v. 29).

Then Christ evaluated the question and judged it irrelevant (v. 30). It was irrelevant because in the resurrection people do not marry. They are similar to angels who do not marry because there is no need to procreate baby angels. The number of the angels was fixed at the time they were created. Similarly, in the afterlife human beings will not marry because there will be no need for infants to be born. Christ was not saying that people become angels after they die, but only that *like* angels they will not procreate. Since that is so, there was no need to answer the Sadducees' question. It was entirely irrelevant. The Levirate marriage law was designed to insure that children would be born to bear the family name of the first dead husband, but in heaven there will be no need for such a provision; hence the irrelevancy of the question.

As if it were not sufficient to charge the Sadducees with error, ignorance, and irrelevance, the Lord proceeded to teach them some sound doctrine from an Old Testament passage (Exodus 3:6), which they considered authoritative. The lesson was simply this: contrary to your doctrine, your Bible teaches that there is life after death. Death does not end it all, as you teach.

Again our Lord used a very sophisticated argument. I expect that few of us would choose to use Exodus 3 to attempt to teach the doctrine of life after death. But our Lord did.

Notice too, just as in John 10:34, He based His argument on the written Word, not general concepts, but specific written words. Specifically, He based His case on how God identified Himself to Moses at the burning bush: "I am the God of Abraham, the God of Isaac, and the God of Jacob." That proves, the Lord went on to say, that God is the God of the living, which means that Abraham, Isaac, and Jacob were still alive though they had died long before those words were spoken.

How does that identification prove the doctrine of life after death? Simply by the use of the present tense, "I am." Abraham, Isaac, and Jacob had died several hundred years before God spoke to Moses. Yet God said that He was still their God at the time He was speaking to Moses. That would not have been possible if when Abraham, Isaac, and Jacob died they ceased to exist. It was only possible if, contrary to the Sadducees' doctrine, death does not end it all.

Of course, the difference between *I am* and *I was* is a matter of verb tense. His argument was based on a present tense rather than a past tense. Christ used the present tense to support the doctrine of resurrection.

The force of what Christ was saying can be il-

69

lustrated this way: Often as a visiting preacher, I am invited home to dinner after the church service by one of the members. I have discovered that usually one of the appropriate topics of conversation is to inquire about the children in that family. Suppose I should ask, "How many children do you have in your family?" And the father or mother replies, "We had four, but one died, so now we only have three." Faced with that kind of response I cannot be very sure about the spiritual condition or maturity of those parents. But if, on the other hand, to the same question another parent replies, "We have four; one is in heaven and three are here with us," then I have a good deal of confidence about that family's beliefs. I can be almost certain that they do not believe that death ends it all but that there is a resurrection coming.

The difference is only in the tense of the verb used: We *had* or we *have*. I *was* their God or I *am* their God.

Observe carefully the ramifications of Christ's statement here.

1. He assumed the historicity of God's appearance to Moses.

2. He assumed that God's revelation came in a propositional statement.

3. He assumed that every word of that statement could be trusted to be precisely accurate.

4. He assumed that doctrinal truth has to be based on historical accuracy. The Bible cannot be inaccurate in matters of history and accurate in doctrine.

5. He assumed that one could use even unlikely passages and trust their accuracy.

Later that same day, when the Pharisees had joined the crowd of antagonists, the Lord became the aggressor, asking a straightforward question of them: "Whose son is the Messiah?" (Matthew

22:41-46). Theirs was an immediate answer: "The son of David." It was correct, but incomplete. Christ is the son of David as far as His humanity is concerned, but He also is the Son of God, and the Lord wanted the Pharisees to acknowledge that as well. So He asked them, "Then how does David in the Spirit call Him Lord?" and to prove that David did, He quoted Psalm 110:1. In that psalm, the Lord (that is, the Father) said to "my Lord" (the Messiah, who was David's Lord), "Sit at my [the Father's] right hand until I [the Father] put Thine [the Messiah's] enemies beneath Thy feet."

How could David call Messiah His Lord if Messiah were only David's son? The only answer is because Messiah was also David's God. In other words the Messiah had to be both God and man. As man He was David's son; as God, David's Lord. The pronoun "my" links David to his Messiah-Lord.

Perhaps an illustration will help. When Queen Elizabeth II dies or abdicates, the Prince of Wales will presumably become King Charles. Assume that Prince Philip, his father, is still living. I ask someone, "King Charles, whose son is he?" The answer would come back: "Prince Philip's." "But," I might reply, "I saw the coronation of King Charles on TV, and I saw Prince Philip bowing and swearing allegiance to him. Why does Philip call Charles 'lord'?" The answer is simple: King Charles is Philip's sovereign—king even though he is also Philip's natural son. He is both Philip's son and Philip's lord. So also Messiah was David's son and, because Messiah is equal with God, He is David's Lord.

Natural procreation links Messiah to David as David's descendant. The pronoun "my" in Psalm 110:1 links Messiah to David as David's Lord God. And the pronoun "my" is simply a *yodh*,

71

that smallest of Hebrew letters, attached to the word "Lord."

There is nothing more central to an orthodox Christology than the full deity and true humanity of Jesus Christ. If He were not the God-man, He could not have been an adequate Savior, high priest, or judge. Who of us would think of using Psalm 110 as our Lord did to emphasize the truth of who He is? But that is exactly what Jesus did, basing his argument with the Pharisees on the single Hebrew word "my Lord." The seeming minutiae of Scripture can be trusted.

What have we learned from our Lord's attitude toward the Bible?

1. The spelling of words can be trusted completely, and not one promise will be fulfilled in any way different from how it was spelled out.

2. The only way the Scripture can lose its authority is if it contains errors, but Christ taught that the Scripture cannot be broken. Thus He must have believed it did not contain errors.

3. The Lord built sophisticated arguments on single words and even the tense of a verb.

Again, I ask, who can say he fully follows the Lord without accepting His teaching concerning the inerrancy of the Scriptures?

Chapter Ten

Our Lord and His Bible

Our Lord
and His Bible

Our Lord had some other things to say about the Bible that showed His absolute confidence in it. His confidence would have been unwarranted if the Bible contained errors.

The Canon. Canon means measuring rod, and thus, metaphorically, a standard. It was first used by Athanasius to refer to those books that measured up to certain standards and were regarded as part of the sacred Scriptures. The criteria used seem clear, and although the results of applying those criteria took some time to emerge, the actual number of books that belong to the canon of the Bible is not generally disputed, with one exception. And that exception, of course, is the Old Testament Apocrypha. It consists of fourteen or fifteen books, depending on whether the letters of Jeremiah and Baruch are separated or counted as one. Written mostly after 200 B.C., the apocryphal books were given various degrees of esteem but were never considered on a par with the canonical Old Testament books until the Roman Catholic church officially pronounced eleven of them canonical at the Council of Trent in 1546.

Our Lord had something to say about the extent of the Old Testament canon, His Bible. When condemning the leaders of the Jews for killing God's messengers throughout history, He charged them with the guilt of shedding the blood of all the righteous from Abel to Zechariah (Matthew 23:35; Luke 11:51). Now the murder of Abel is recorded in Genesis 4, and the murder of Zechariah is found in 2 Chronicles 24, which in the arrangement of the Hebrew canon was the last book in order (as is Malachi in our arrangement). In other words, the Lord was saying in effect, "From the first to the last murder in the Bible." There were, of course, other murders recorded in apocryphal books, but the Lord does not choose to include those in those He cites. Apparently, He did not consider those apocryphal books to be of equal authority with the books from Genesis to 2 Chronicles. Thus in one statement He let everyone know what He considered the canonical Old Testament Scriptures.

His temptation. The account of the temptation of our Lord reveals some important matters concerning His view of the Bible.

1. Jesus accepted the plenary inspiration of the Bible. When first approached by the devil to turn stones into bread, our Lord replied that man lives by *every word* that proceeds from the mouth of God. (Matthew 4:4, quoting Deuteronomy 8:3). He did not say "some things" but "every thing." If Scripture is breathed out from God (2 Timothy 3:16), then Scripture must be included in what sustains man, not only parts of Scripture but all of it.

76

The second temptation also illustrates the importance of plenary inspiration. Satan tried to entice the Lord to throw Himself off the pinnacle of the Temple by assuring Him that He could claim the promise of Psalm 91:11-12 that God's angels would guard Him. But in quoting those verses Satan omitted part of verse 11: "To guard you in all your ways." The omission distorts the meaning of the promise, which is that God will keep the righteous on their journeys, not that He will preserve them when they take needless risks. A needless risk was exactly what Satan had proposed to Christ. The Lord replied that to bank on part of a verse would be to tempt God. Instead He would rely on *every* word that came from God, including every word of Psalm 91:11-12.

2. Jesus accepted the truth of the propositions of the Bible. As has been said, a popular viewpoint today sees the Bible as containing only personal revelation, not propositional revelation. That is, the Bible reveals God and Christ accurately, but it does so in a person-to-person relationship rather than in statements. Therefore, although we can trust the message of the Bible, we really cannot (nor do we need to) trust the particular statements or propositions of the Bible. The Bible, this view says, witnesses to the infallible truth, but it does not have to do so with inerrant statements. The pointer, the Bible, is fallible, but Christ, to whom it points, is infallible.

But Christ's response to Satan's attacks negates that viewpoint. He said, "It is written" (Matthew 4:4, 7, 10). He did not say, "It witnesses." He relied on propositional statements to convey truth in and of themselves and to convey it accurately.

The history in the Old Testament. Our Lord used historical incidents in the Old Testament in a manner that evinced His total confidence in their factual historicity.

1. He acknowledged that Adam and Eve were created by God, that they were two living human beings, not merely symbols of mankind and womankind, and that they acted in specific ways (Matthew 19:3-5; Mark 10:6-8).

2. He verified events connected with the Flood of Noah's day; namely, that there was an ark and that the Flood destroyed everyone who was not in that ark (Matthew 24:38-39; Luke 17:26-27).

3. On two different occasions, He authenticated God's destruction of Sodom, and the historicity of Lot and his wife (Matthew 10:15, 23; Luke 17:28-29).

4. He accepted as true the story of Jonah and the great fish (Matthew 12:40).

5. He acknowledged the historicity of Isaiah (Matthew 12:17), Elijah (Matthew 17:11-12), Daniel (Matthew 24:15), Abel (Matthew 23:35), Zechariah (Matthew 23:35), Abiathar (Mark 2:26), David (Matthew 22:45), Moses and his writings (Matthew 8:4; John 5:46), Abraham, Isaac, and Jacob (Matthew 8:11; John 8:39).

Some very important conclusions must be drawn:

1. Christ did not merely *allude* to those stories, but He also *authenticated* the events in them as factual history to be completely trusted.

2. Those events include many of the controversial passages of the Old Testament—creation, the Flood, the major miracles including Jonah and the fish.

Obviously, our Lord felt He had a reliable Bible, historically true, with every word trustworthy.

Chapter Eleven

Some Problems in the Old Testament

Some Problems in the Old Testament

No one denies that there are passages in the Bible that contain problems of one kind or another. The inerrancy question does not involve interpretive problems or debates concerning the best text type. But problems of apparent discrepancies, conflicting numbers, differences in parallel accounts, or allegedly unscientific statements do concern the inerrancy of the Bible.

Errantists and inerrantists have access to the same facts concerning each of those problems. Both have capable minds to use in interacting with those facts. Both can read the conclusions of others. But both do not come to those problems with the same basic outlook. The errantist's outlook includes not only the possibility but also the reality of errors in the Bible. Therefore, when he studies problems, one of his possible conclusions is that one or another of them is actually an error.

The inerrantist, on the other hand, has concluded that the Bible contains no errors. Therefore, he exercises no option to conclude that any of those same problems is an example of a genuine error in the Bible. His research may lead him to conclude that some problem is yet unexplainable. Nevertheless, he believes it is not an error and that either further research will demonstrate that or he will understand the solution in heaven.

Consider this illustration: If a happily married man comes home unexpectedly one day to find his wife waving good-bye to a handsome man about to get into a car, what will he think? If his confidence and trust in his wife is total and unwavering because of their years of satisfying experiences together, he will assume she had a good reason for seeing that man. Though he may be curious, the husband will not doubt his wife's loyalty. Perhaps it will not be until Christmas or their anniversary that he learns that the man he saw was delivering a special present his wife had ordered for him.

But if his confidence in his relationship with his wife is even a bit shaky, his thoughts will wander into all kinds of paths including suspicion of unfaithfulness on her part. Because of his insecurity, his wife might be branded an adulteress in his eyes.

The analogy is clear, is it not? If I come to the Bible with confidence that its words were breathed out from God and are therefore without errors, and if that confidence has been buttressed by years of proving the Bible totally reliable, then I will not be shaken by a problem, and I certainly will not conclude that it is an error. But if I think there can be errors in the Bible, however few or many, then I will likely conclude that some of those problems are examples of errors. And even

82

if there is only one, I have an errant Bible.

From the current literature on the inerrancy debate, it is difficult to cull a definitive list of "errors." It is probably not possible to list criteria by which to judge errors, only to list actual examples of errors. Although no two writers agree on a list of errors, when all the examples are put together there are about two dozen, more or less.

The lack of uniformity in those lists raises a serious question: Who and what determines the boundary line between the territory of permissable errancy and the territory of necessary inerrancy? If, for instance, some errancy can be expected and tolerated in historical matters, but not in doctrinal areas, how do I know *which* historical matters? After all, some important doctrines are built on historical matters. So where do I draw the line?

Admittedly, there are certain problem passages to examine. However, I maintain that reasonable suggestions can be found so that we need not conclude they are errors.

In a discussion like this I can only make suggestions, and not in great detail. Further information is readily available in other books and commentaries. But the point is that suggestions have been made that are compatible with the doctrine of inerrancy.

The "two accounts" of creation. Although the allegation that there are two conflicting accounts of creation has ramifications in a number of areas of interpretation, often in the inerrancy discussion the focus is on the supposed contradiction between Genesis 1:11-12, which records vegetation appearing on the third day, and Genesis 2:5, which seems to say there was no vegetation until after Adam was created.

Two things are wrong about such a conclusion. First, Genesis 2 adds details to the account of creation in Genesis 1, not in contradiction but in supplementation. For example, 1:27 says that God created man (a generic term here) male and female, but not meaning that the first creature was a male-female combination. The details of that creation of the male Adam and the female Eve are given in 2:18-23. Likewise, Genesis 2:5 adds details about the creation of vegetation on the third day.

Second, the words used in 2:5 refer to the kind of plants that require cultivation, not to all kinds of green plants. Plants that required such cultivation either did not appear until Adam was created and could then cultivate them, or they appeared but did not grow until Adam was created.

H. C. Leupold has summed up the matter well: Verse 4*b* takes us back into the time of the work of creation, more particularly to the time before the work of the third day began, and draws our attention to certain details, which, being details, could hardly have been inserted in chapter one: the fact that certain forms of life, namely the kinds that require the attentive care of man in greater measure, had not sprung up. . . . When verdure covered the earth, the sprouting of these types of vegetation was retarded, so that they might appear after man was already in full possession of his domain and in a position to give them their needed care. . . . The fact that not the whole of vegetation is meant appears from the distinctive terms employed, neither of which had as yet appeared in the account. . . . From all this it appears sufficiently how absurd the claim is that in this account (chapter 2:4 ff) man is made first, then vegetation. [H. C. Leupold, *Exposition of Genesis* (Columbus, Ohio: Wartburg,

1942), pp. 112-13.]

Thus a contradiction and therefore an error appears in this account only for those who want it. Good exegesis requires no error.

Cain's wife. Though by many inerrantists the question of where Cain got his wife would not be considered a problem at all, the question is often used by those who try to demonstrate that the Bible is unreliable in what it claims. How could it claim that Adam and Eve were the first human beings who had two sons, one of whom murdered the other, and yet who produced a large race of people? Clearly, the Bible does teach that Adam and Eve were the first created human beings. The Lord affirmed that in Matthew 19:3-9. The genealogy of Christ is traced back to Adam (Luke 3:38). Jude 14 identifies Enoch as the seventh from Adam. That could hardly mean the seventh from "mankind," an interpretation that would be necessary if Adam were not an individual, as some claim. Clearly, Cain murdered Abel and yet many people were born. Where did Cain get his wife?

We know that Adam and Eve had other sons and daughters in addition to Abel, Cain, and Seth (Genesis 5:4), and if there was only one original family, then the first marriages had to be between brothers and sisters.

Such marriages in the beginning were not harmful. Incest is dangerous because inherited mutant genes that produce deformed, sickly, or mentally retarded children are more likely to find expression in children if those genes are carried by both parents. Certainly Adam and Eve, coming from the creative hand of God, had no such mutant genes. Therefore, marriages between brothers and sisters or nieces or nephews in the first and second generations following Adam and

Eve would not have been dangerous.

Numbers 25:9. The plague that followed Israel's worship of Baal of Peor killed 24,000 people according to Moses. Yet Paul records only 23,000 deaths in 1 Corinthians 10:8. An obvious error? Not necessarily, for Paul limits his 23,000 figure to those killed on one day. The account in Numbers 25 records that the judges were involved in carrying out the judgment and may include additional deaths that occurred the following days. In other words, they may not have completed their awesome task in one day. The two accounts do not conflict because of Paul's additional phrase "in one day."

But no damage is done to inerrancy if we consider both numbers as round figures. If so, then the number killed was between 23,000 and 24,000. If either passage stated that "exactly" or "only" a certain number died, and if they did not agree, then that would constitute a clear error. But such is not the case.

Who caused David to number Israel (2 Samuel 24:1 and 1 Chronicles 21:1)? One account says the Lord did, whereas the other says Satan did. But why does that have to be a conflict? Could not both the Lord and Satan have been involved? They have been in other matters. Paul said that the Lord sent a messenger to Satan to keep him from exalting himself (2 Corinthians 12:7). Certainly the Lord and Satan are involved in activities that lead to Armageddon. Why not here also? Such a simple solution makes even the suggestion of a contradiction seem incredible. Yet this is no straw man. One errantist emphatically stated that "both accounts cannot be accurate. But from the viewpoint of doctrinal integrity they both present exactly the same truth: What David did was wrong. . ." (Ray Summers, *The Baptist Standard,* 4 February 1970, p. 12).

Who killed Goliath (2 Samuel 21:19 compared with 1 Samuel 17:50)? Did David kill Goliath or did someone else, named Elhanan? Before assuming that the accounts are in conflict and therefore that one is in error, let us ask some other questions: (a) Could David have had two names, the other one being Elhanan? Solomon had two names (2 Samuel 12:24-25). (b) Could there have been two Goliaths? In the immediate context (v. 20), another giant at Gath is mentioned. (c) Perhaps we are to understand that Elhanan killed the brother of Goliath. Any of those solutions is equally plausible; it is unnecessary to conclude the presence of an error. And all of them are more plausible in light of the proved accuracy of the Bible elsewhere.

Certain numbers in 2 Samuel 24 and 1 Chronicles 21. Other numbers in these parallel accounts seem not to harmonize, and errantists conclude that some things are in error. Second Samuel 24:9 says 800,000 were numbered in Israel and 500,000 in Judah, whereas 2 Chronicles 21:5 gives a 1,100,000 total for Israel and 470,000 for Judah. The difference in the total for Israel may be accounted for by assuming that the 800,000 figure did not include the 300,000 listed in 1 Chronicles 27, which if added would make a total equal to the 1,100,000 figure in 1 Chronicles 21:5. Perhaps the 30,000 difference in the other figures involves the 30,000 specially mentioned in 2 Samuel 6:1.

When God gave David a choice of punishment, He offered as an option seven years of famine according to 2 Samuel 24:13 and three years famine according to 1 Chronicles 21:12. The Septuagint translation says three years, so likely the figure in 2 Samuel is a scribal error. Though copies were very carefully made, errors inevitably crept in. This seems to be one, but it is not an error in the original—that was inerrant when it was written. Regrettably, inerrancy cannot be extended to the copies.

Finally, in these chapters the question of how much David paid for the property he bought from Araunah seems to be in conflict in the two accounts. Second Samuel 24:24 says 50 shekels of silver, but 1 Chronicles 21:25 records 600 shekels as the price. The difference is great, even allowing for inflation! But is it too great if, as 2 Samuel 24:24 says, the 50 shekels were paid for the threshing floor alone whereas the larger amount included other property surrounding it?

The laver in 2 Chronicles 4:2. In describing the measurements of the laver, the circumference is given as thirty cubits (or 540 inches if the cubit was 18 inches) and the diameter is ten cubits (180 inches). However, circumference is arrived at by multiplying the diameter by pi (3.14159), and that total is more than 565 inches, an apparent contradiction. One writer resolves the problem by saying that "in the culture of the day the measurement was not only accurate, but also 'inerrant.' " (Robert Mounce, "Clues to Understanding Biblical Accuracy," *Eternity,* June 1966, p. 18).

However, there is a better solution that does not include sleight of hand. The ten-cubit measurement was from brim to brim; that is from one outside edge to the other. But verse 5 states that the width of the edge was a handbreadth, or about 4 inches. So the inside diameter was ten cubits (180 inches) minus two handbreadths (8 inches). Multiplying 172 inches by pi, the total is 540 inches, the same circumference as given in verse 2.

Those represent passages currently being used as illustrations of errors in the Old Testament. Without going into great detail I have tried to show that reasonable explanations are at hand.

We need not conclude that errors are present in the text except for, possibly, occasional copyists' errors. How one views those suggestions will be a reflection of one's underlying confidence, or lack of it, in the Bible itself.

Chapter Twelve

Some Problems in the New Testament

Some Problems in the New Testament

Errantists also cite a number of passages from the New Testament that supposedly deny inerrancy or at least require a definition of inerrancy that contains so much latitude that it becomes errancy. One writer cites 2 Chronicles 4:2, Numbers 25:9, Mark 2:26, and Matthew 22:42 as examples of "a kind of inerrancy that falls short of perfect conformity to what was actually said" and of problems to which only "highly fanciful" explanations could be given (Robert Mounce, "Clues to Understanding Biblical Accuracy," *Eternity*, June 1966, p. 18).

Another is troubled by Matthew 13:31-32 and problems in Acts 7 that he says cannot be solved compatibly with inerrancy (Daniel P. Fuller, "Evangelicalism and Biblical Inerrancy" [unpublished material, 1966], pp. 18-19). Still another cites Matthew 27:9 as an error and says that there are "hundreds of examples like this one" (Berkeley Mickelsen, "The Bible's Own Approach to Authority," in Jack B. Rogers, ed., *Biblical Authority* [Waco, Tex.: Word, 1977], p. 86). We cannot obviously discuss "hundreds" of unnamed examples, but we will look at the ones named in the writings of those who hold to something less than total inerrancy.

Matthew 10:9-10 (Mark 6:8; Luke 9:3). Matthew records that Jesus allowed the disciples to take staffs, whereas Mark and Luke say He forbade doing so. That leads one errantist to say: "I know of no way to reconcile this inconsistency. The proper conclusion, I think, is that the accounts are inconsistent and that at least one of the Gospels is in error" (Stephen T. Davis, *The Debate about the Bible* [Philadelphia: Westminster, 1977], p. 106).

If one believes that every word of the text was inspired, then he would surely notice that in Mark and Luke the verb is the same and means that they should take the staffs they already possess. Matthew uses a different verb, which means that the disciples were not to procure staffs. Putting the accounts together, the Lord permitted them to take along the staffs they already owned, but prohibited procuring new or additional ones.

Notice that errancy feeds on itself. If all the words cannot be trusted, then one may tend not to do careful exegesis and therefore either ignore or refuse to accept a perfectly proper grammatical explanation like this one.

Matthew 13:32. In His parable of the mustard seed the Lord said that the mustard seed was the smallest of all the seeds. Is that plainly an erroneous statement since botanically the mustard seed is not the smallest? Before jumping to that conclusion, remember that it was stated by Jesus Christ. If He spoke a lie, how could He have been sinless? This is not simply a small factual discrepancy; if the statement is not true, then it proves something about the one who made it, and that becomes a serious doctrinal matter. You cannot separate this history from its doctrinal ramification.

But how are we to understand the Lord's words? One suggestion stated well by R. C. Trench years ago is this: "This seed, when cast into the ground, is *'the least of all seeds,'*—words which have often perplexed interpreters, many seeds, as of poppy or rue, being smaller. Yet difficulties of this kind are not worth making; it is sufficient to know that 'small as a grain of mustard-seed' was a proverbial expression among the Jews for something exceedingly minute (see Luke xvii. 6). The Lord, in His popular teaching, adhered to the popular language" (R. C. Trench, *Notes on the Parables of Our Lord* [New York: Revell, n.d.], p. 91).

Another fact to note is that the word *smallest* is actually a comparative not a superlative, and should be translated (as in the *New American Standard Bible* and *New English Bible*), "smaller of all the seeds." In other words, the Lord did not state an absolute (the mustard seed is absolutely the smallest), but placed the mustard seed in the class of smallest seeds.

Perhaps the two suggestions should be combined. Technically, He placed the mustard seed among the smaller seeds and capitalized on the popular proverbial understanding of that seed as representing something exceedingly minute. But He did not make a technical or scientific error.

The blind men at Jericho (Matthew 20:29-34; Mark 10:46-52; Luke 18:35-43). The accounts of the healing of the blind men at Jericho (one of them being Bartimaeus) contain some different details that some have interpreted as irresolvable, leading to the conclusion that one or another of the accounts must contain errors. Matthew says that the Lord healed two blind men as He left Jericho. The other accounts mention only one blind man and record the miracle being performed as they entered Jericho. As to the number of blind men, if Mark or Luke had said *only* one blind man, then there would be an error. But if Bartimaeus was the more forward of the two, then it would be natural for one writer to focus on him, whereas another might mention both of them. The statement that there were two includes the focus on one. A statement that there were two would conflict if there were a statement that there was only one. But such is not the case.

As to when the miracle happened, two plausible suggestions have been made. One is that the men pleaded with the Lord as He entered Jericho, but were not healed until He was leaving. The other is that since there were two Jerichos (old Jericho and the new city), the healing could have taken place after the group left old Jericho and as they were nearing new Jericho. Thus Matthew's "as they were going out" refers to old Jericho, whereas Mark's and Luke's references to approaching Jericho refer to new Jericho.

Whichever suggestion is adopted, it is clear that there is no need to see an insoluble contradiction in those accounts.

Matthew 23:35. In this verse Zechariah (not the prophet by the same name, but a priest) is said to be the son of Berechiah, but in 2 Chronicles 24:20 he is said to be the son of Jehoiada. "Son of" does not have to mean the next immediate generation, (as in Genesis 31:28 where Laban refers to his grandchildren as sons and daughters, or as in the case of Christ, the son of David and Abraham, Matthew 1:1). Most likely, Jehoiada was Zechariah's grandfather and is named in the Chronicles account because of his fame.

Matthew 27:9-10. The main part of this quotation comes from Zechariah 11:12-13, whereas Matthew seems to ascribe it to Jeremiah. Is this not a clear mistake on Matthew's part?

Before reaching such a conclusion, consider that Jeremiah was placed at the beginning of the Old Testament prophetic writings in the Babylonian Talmud. Matthew, then, may be simply using Jeremiah's name to designate the section of the Old Testament from which the Zechariah references come. It is much like saying, "In the book by Smith, Jones said . . ." Jones wrote a chapter in a book that Smith edited. (This is not to suggest, however, that Jeremiah edited Zechariah's prophecy). Note the same prominence given Jeremiah in Matthew 16:14, where he is the only prophet named specifically though others are included in the statement.

Though that seems the most plausible explanation, some find a solution in the thought that Matthew had primarily in mind the events mentioned about the potter's house in Jeremiah 18 and 19.

Mark 1:2-3. These verses raise a problem since immediately after the words "as it is written in Isaiah the prophet," there follows a quotation from Malachi, then a quotation from Isaiah. Many regard this as an obvious error, though a harmless one. However, the structure of the chapter introduces the "beginning of the gospel" by focusing on the ministry of John the Baptist in the wilderness. So the quotation from Isaiah is in Mark's mind the principal one because it predicted the figure in the wilderness. His attention's being on the Isaiah prophecy explains why he mentions Isaiah only in verse two.

Mark 2:26. Mark, in referring to David's eating the Tabernacle bread, says Abiathar was the high priest, whereas the Old Testament record of this event states that Ahimelech was (1 Samuel 21:1-6). A solution recognizes that although the

97

event actually happened during Ahimelech's priesthood, he soon was killed, and Abiathar, who also would have been exercising priestly functions at that time, shortly became high priest and proved to be more prominent than Ahimelech. Mark is not saying that Abiathar was actually high priest when the event took place, but he was a ministering priest and soon became a very prominent high priest. Similarly one might speak of some event that occurred in the senatorial years of John F. Kennedy and refer to it as happening in the days of Kennedy, the president. He was not president when it happened, rather a senator, but he is identified as Kennedy the president because he (later) became a prominent president.

Again, the examples in Mark remind us that if someone comes to the Bible expecting or allowing for error, he can make a case for an errant Scripture. But if he comes expecting the Bible to be inerrant, he can find plausible solutions, and even if he cannot honestly accept any of the suggested solutions, he can still believe that the Bible is inerrant and that we simply do not yet have enough facts to solve some of the problems.

The death of Judas. In Acts 1:18, Peter describes Judas' death as "falling headlong, he burst open in the middle and all his bowels gushed out." Matthew says that Judas hanged himself (Matthew 27:5). Most likely both descriptions are true. He did hang himself but something happened that caused his body to fall and break open. This is the simplest solution and has been suggested since the time of Augustine.

The same two accounts seem to contain another problem. Matthew states that the priests bought the "field of blood," whereas Acts attributes it to Judas. Again the simple solution is that both accounts are correct. The priests could not take the money back, so they bought the field in Judas' name since they did not want to appear to have anything to do with his money.

Problems in Acts 7. Although it is well within the boundaries of the concept of inerrancy to permit Stephen in this speech to utter something erroneous and have Luke record it accurately, the serious interpreter will want to know as clearly as possible what Stephen was saying. One of the problems focuses on verse 6 where Stephen gives the length of the Egyptian captivity as 400 years, whereas Exodus 12:40 says 430 years. Further, Paul in Galatians 3:17 wrote that the law came 430 years after the Abrahamic promise. The problems in those figures are two: (a) The difference between 400 and 430, and (b) the apparently large error of Paul, because the time between Abraham and the giving of the law was considerably longer than 430 years. Many simply acknowledge that the 400/430 difference involves an approximation. Four hundred is 430 rounded off. The 430 years in Galatians does not use the termini from Abraham to the law (Genesis 12 to Exodus 20). Rather, it refers to the end of the patriarchal age (Genesis 35:11-12) to the giving of the law in Exodus 20.

Others believe that 400 years was the duration of the Egyptian bondage and that both 430-year figures refer to the time between the last confirmation of the Abrahamic covenant to Jacob and the giving of the law. This illustrates a case where we simply do not have enough known facts to be able to make a conclusive decision. So once again one's attitude comes into play: you can believe there are errors, or you can believe that there would be perfect resolution if all the facts were known.

Sometimes the apparent problem in verse 14 poses a question. There Jacob's family is said to be seventy-five persons, whereas in Genesis

46:27 only seventy are included. Stephen in Acts follows the Septuagint number, which included five extra persons (the son and grandson of Manasseh and two sons and grandson of Ephraim). Genesis does not include those. But in both numbers only a restricted group is included because the total number of the family of Jacob would have been much greater, including wives of Jacob's sons and grandsons and husbands of his daughters and granddaughters who are not listed. Anyone trying to list the number in an immediate family of that size would easily have come up with at least two ways of doing it and two different totals without contradiction.

Those represent the New Testament problems being discussed. Some of them have been used throughout church history to try to prove that there are errors in the Bible. And reasonable solutions to the problems have been proposed throughout history. Some have come into focus more recently. Any of them might be used to conclude that the Bible contains errors, but all of them do have reasonable explanations.

Remember, it takes only one error to make an errant Bible. It may be a "small" error, an inconsequential one, an historical one, or a doctrinal one, but if there is one, then we do not have an inerrant Bible.

Chapter Thirteen

Important Ramifications

Important Ramifications

No one can predict with total accuracy what doctrinal dominoes may topple after inerrancy falls. Defections do not always follow a logical pattern. Nevertheless, some general predictions can be made as to what may happen when inerrancy goes.

That is not to say that everyone who may hold to one or more of these deviations I am going to list denies inerrancy, nor am I saying that such a denial inevitably brings these deviations, but some or all of them will probably be evident whenever inerrancy is abandoned.

Deviations in the area of the supernatural. It is a historical fact that a less than total view of inerrancy has resulted in a denial of some or all of the miracles of the Bible. Usually Old Testament miracles are the first either to be denied outright or explained as happening naturally rather than supernaturally. Often the attack is directed against the historical events recorded in the first eleven chapters of Genesis. That means that the accounts of creation or of the sin of man or of the Flood are denied as being historically and factually true. The direct attack calls them myths with no factual content. Less frontally, some try to maintain the "truth" of the stories while denying the factual and historical content (a neat sleight-of-hand kind of exegesis!). They say, for example, that nothing could be more truthful than the fact of sin, but, of course, no persons named Adam and Eve ever lived at any time in history in an actual place called Eden to commit that first sin. But by either the direct or less direct routes, the result is the same—the events did not happen historically, and therefore many biblical passages are erroneous.

If that seems to be too strong a statement, remember that other parts of the Bible refer to the events in Genesis 1-11 as historically true. For instance, aspects of the account of creation and the Fall are affirmed in Exodus 20:11, 1 Chronicles 1:1, Job 31:33, Hosea 6:7, Matthew 19:4, Mark 10:6, Luke 3:38, Romans 5:14, 1 Corinthians 11:9; 15:22, 45; 2 Corinthians 11:3; 1 Timothy 2:13-14; and Jude 14.

Abandonment of inerrancy and a naturalistic explanation of miracles frequently go hand in hand. The plagues in Egypt often furnish a good example. From there it is a short step to denying the supernatural aspect of the miracles of Christ. Errancy allows for that and may even encourage it.

Underlying those denials in the realm of the supernatural is the errantist's use of the historical-critical method of understanding Scripture. The method is based on liberal presuppositions about the Bible, so that when evangelicals use it, those presuppositions inevitably rub off. They include: (a) nothing can be accepted as God's Word unless it can be proved to be so; (b) man's reason sits in judgment on the Bible to decide what is God's Word and what is not; (c) therefore what man's reason decides to be God's Word is accepted, and what man judges not to be God's Word is rejected.

Apply that methodology to the question of creation and here is the result: unless one can prove the creationist's view of Genesis, one says it cannot be God's Word; the mind, filled with the teachings of evolution, judges what part of Genesis is true and what is to be reinterpreted to harmonize with scientific claims. Such a person concludes that Adam and Eve were not necessarily the first parents, if indeed they existed at all, and certainly the whole process could not have been accomplished in anything less than very long ages of time.

Apply the same method to angels and demons. Such beings are incompatible with reason and science, so the mind concludes that they cannot exist and that passages that teach they do are either in error or accommodate to the ignorances of the people of the times.

Apply the historical-critical method to certain historical sections of the Bible that errantists see as containing errors. Their intellectual investigations lead them to the conclusion that there are errors in some of those portions of the Bible, therefore, those portions cannot have the same authority as other parts. The contemporary errantist says that makes little difference, for those errors are in nonrevelational sections of the Bible, which do not affect our doctrine or practice. The revelational sections are inerrant, and that is what really matters to our faith.

But who decides which sections are revelational and which are not? The interpreter. In other words, the contemporary errantist divides Scripture into sections that affect faith, and particularly salvation, and sections that do not. He employs a method similar to that used by the historical-critical method liberals. Of course the evangelical errantist does not embrace all of the same conclusions the liberal does, and he considers the Bible to be more authoritative; but that evangelical is on the same slide, though he may not have gone as far or as fast.

Deviations in the area of sex. Comtemporary society has shown its tolerance in varying degrees toward adultery, homosexuality, abortion, and divorce. That serves as a challenge to the authority of the Bible. It also may weaken the stand of those who acknowledge the presence of errors in the Bible because it so clearly violates biblical imperatives.

One writer asserts that women had certain rights before Christianity. She says that one way to restore the equality that Christianity has denied women is to assume that there are two conflicting accounts of creation in Genesis. She shifts the emphasis to the account in Genesis 1 where both man and women were said to be created at the same time and thus with equality. Such an interpretation clearly denies inerrancy and is used in this case to justify a permissiveness that the Bible clearly does not allow (Virginia Ramey Mollenkott, "The Women's Movement," *Journal of Psychology and Theology* 2, no. 4 [Fall 1974]: 307-8).

Deviations in the area of subordination. Could errancy and some of its deviations be symptomatic of a deeper problem, the problem of subordination? Clearly God has set up certain hierarchies in the Scriptures that are violated by permissive teachings on homosexuality, abortion, and some aspects of the role of women in the church. Similar insubordination shows up in the contemporary doctrine of "selective obedience" toward the laws of government. (The position might just as well be labeled "selective disobedience".) Not only did we see that in relation to the draft and going to war, but we continue to see it in relation to other laws that some judge as not good and therefore feel free to disobey. The authoritative teaching of Romans 13 and 1 Peter 2 does not allow that attitude.

May I insert a word of caution to my fellow inerrantists? We must be very careful that our hermeneutics or artificial exegesis do not lead us to a practical denial of inerrancy by diminishing the authority of passages to which we apply such exegesis. If we do not think God straightforwardly says what He means, then we do not have to acknowledge that He means what He says.

Where will all this lead? Some apparently can hold a reasonably high view of Scripture and its authority while denying its total inerrancy. Others have moved far away from a conservative view of the Bible, denying the historicity of some of its passages, diluting the miraculous, accepting some of the conclusions of the historical-critical method of interpretation, and replacing divine authority with human, existential, subjective authority. Many are somewhere in between.

Consider this illustration: There are two sausage factories in a town. When you go into one of the plants you see that everything is spotlessly clean. As you watch the process you see the workers mixing the sausage ingredients. Accidentially, one of them drops a handful of meat on the floor. He quickly reaches down and picks it up and throws it in the trash. Then he immediately scrubs the area of the floor where the meat fell until it is spotless again. In due time, the sausage comes out, is packaged, stamped Grade A, is sold, and when eaten it nourishes people.

You then visit the other factory. It, too, appears quite clean. Again you watch the workers mixing the ingredients. A similar accident happens, and one of the workers drops something on the floor. This time, however, he picks up the meat and puts it back into the mixer along with the rest. He reaches down and swipes at the floor with a rag pulled from his hip pocket. The process continues, the sausage is finished, packaged, stamped Grade A, sold, eaten, and it nourishes people.

The sausage from both plants meets government standards, and all of it is nourishing. But let me ask two questions. First, which brand would you prefer to buy? Obviously, the one made in the spotlessly clean plant would be more desirable. The other might not hurt you, but on the other hand, something may have gotten into it due to uncleanliness. Eating it could make you sick. Who could be sure that a little dirt in sausage—or a little error in the Bible—will not harm the user?

Before asking the second question, let me add a few more details to the illustration. The less than spotless plant is family owned. The sons are being trained to take over the family business, and part of that training, whether by design or default, permits them to put ingredients that have fallen on the floor back into the machine. The father watches things rather closely, but not perfectly. Now the second question: When the sons take over, what will be their standards? More strict than their father's? Or more lenient? Most likely more lenient, and more and more so as time passes. Finally, one day their product will fail to meet even government standards, and they will be out of business.

What of the Bible's future? Perhaps the parable of the two sausage factories gives us a clue.

Errantists today are communicating what they believe to some circle of followers and are *affecting* people in those circles. Errantist professors affect their students who affect their churches who affect their denominations. Errantist writers plant seeds of doubt in the minds of their readers, assuring them they can have their cake (the authority of the Bible) and eat it too (the errors in the Bible). All of that not only battles for the minds of the present generation, but spills over on the next generation of teachers, preachers, and laymen. The lines are drawn. Where do you stand?